Manchester United

Trivia

Quizzes, Fun Facts, and Challenges for Every Red Devils Fan

CONTENT

Part 1: Introduction to Manchester United FC Football

Chapter 1: History of Formation

Chapter 2: Development and Legacy

Chapter 3: Global Fanbase

Part 2: Famous Players of Manchester United FC Football

Chapter 1: The Legends

Chapter 2: Modern-Day Stars

Chapter 3: Key Achievements

Part 3: Games

Chapter 1: True-False Questions

Chapter 2: Trivia Questions

Chapter 3: Fill-in-the-Blank & Other Games

Part 1: Introduction to Manchester United FC Football

Chapter 1: History of Formation

Early Days as Newton Heath (1878-1902)

Manchester United's story begins in 1878, not with the globally recognized name, but as Newton Heath LYR Football Club. Founded by the carriage and wagon department of the Lancashire and Yorkshire Railway depot in Newton Heath, the club initially played friendly matches against other railway departments and companies. Their first recorded match took place on November 20, 1880, a 6-0 defeat to Bolton Wanderers' reserve team.

Newton Heath gradually became more competitive, joining The Combination, a regional football league, in 1888. They turned professional in 1889 and entered the Football League in 1892. However, success was elusive, and financial troubles plagued the club at the turn of the century.

To truly understand Manchester United's origins, we need to delve deeper into those formative years as Newton Heath LYR Football Club. Here's a closer look at their early days:

- **Humble Beginnings:** Formed in 1878 by railway workers, the club was initially a source of recreation and camaraderie amongst colleagues. They played on a field near the railway depot on North Road, their early matches consisting of friendly games against other railway departments.

- **Early Organization and Growth:** While initially casual, the club soon showed signs of organization. A committee was formed, and they began competing in local cup competitions. In 1888, Newton Heath joined The Combination, a regional league that provided more structured competition.

- **Turning Professional and Joining the Football League:** A significant step came in 1889 when Newton Heath turned professional. This allowed them to attract better players and compete at a higher level. In 1892, they were elected to the newly formed Football League First Division, a testament to their growing ambition.

- **Challenges and Struggles:** Life in the First Division proved challenging for the young club. They faced strong competition and struggled to maintain their position. Relegation to the Second Division followed in 1894. Financial difficulties were a constant concern, with the club relying heavily on the support of the railway company and fundraising efforts.

- **The Bank Street Ground:** In 1893, Newton Heath moved to a new ground on Bank Street in Clayton. While an improvement from their previous field, the Bank Street ground was located next to a chemical works, and the polluted air often made for difficult playing conditions.

- **Key Figures:** Several individuals played crucial roles in Newton Heath's early years. **James McNaught** was the club's first captain, while **Alfred Harold Albut** served as chairman for many years, guiding the club through its early challenges. **Harry Stafford**, the club secretary, would later play a pivotal role in the club's transformation into Manchester United.

- **The Colors:** Newton Heath's original colors were green and gold, a far cry from the famous red of Manchester United. These colors have been revived in recent years by fan groups protesting against the club's ownership.

The End of an Era:

By the end of the 19th century, Newton Heath LYR FC was a club facing an uncertain future. Despite their efforts, on-field success remained elusive, and financial problems loomed large. The club was on the verge of bankruptcy, setting the stage for a dramatic rescue and a new beginning

A New Name and Early Successes (1902-1915)

On the brink of bankruptcy in 1902, the club was rescued by local brewer John Henry Davies. He, along with four other businessmen, invested in the club and changed its name to Manchester United. This marked a turning point. Under the management of Ernest Mangnall, United won its first major trophy, the FA Cup, in 1909. This was followed by the club's first league title in 1908 and another in 1911.

In 1910, Manchester United moved to its now-famous home, Old Trafford. The stadium, with an initial capacity of 80,000, was a symbol of the club's growing ambition.

The renaming to Manchester United in 1902 truly signaled a fresh start and a period of growth for the club. Here's a closer look at those early triumphs:

- John Henry Davies and the New Investment: John Henry Davies, a wealthy local brewer, stepped in to rescue the club from financial ruin. He not only provided much-needed funds but also brought a sense of ambition and a desire to see Manchester United succeed at the highest level.

- Ernest Mangnall - The Architect of Success: Davies appointed Ernest Mangnall as manager in 1903. Mangnall proved to be an inspired choice. He was a shrewd tactician and a strong motivator who built a competitive squad and instilled a winning mentality.

- First Taste of Glory: In 1908, Manchester United achieved a historic milestone by winning their first league title. This victory announced their arrival as a major force in English football and brought the club its first taste of significant silverware.

- FA Cup Triumph: The following year, in 1909, Manchester United added the FA Cup to their trophy cabinet. This victory further solidified their status as one of the top teams in the country and fueled the growing enthusiasm of their supporters.

- Old Trafford - A New Home: In 1910, Manchester United moved into their now-iconic home, Old Trafford. With a capacity of 80,000, it was one of the largest stadiums in the country and a symbol of the club's ambition.

- Star Players: This era saw the emergence of some of the club's early legends, including Billy Meredith, Sandy Turnbull, and Harold Halse. These players were instrumental in United's success, their skill and determination captivating the fans.

- Developing an Identity: Under Mangnall's guidance, Manchester United developed an attractive, attacking style of play that emphasized speed and passing. This helped to establish a distinct identity for the club and attracted a growing fanbase.

End of the First Golden Era:

While the period from 1902 to 1915 was a time of great success, the outbreak of World War I brought an abrupt halt to the club's progress. Many players enlisted in the armed forces, and football leagues were suspended. However, the foundations had been laid for future success, and the club had established itself as a major force in English football.

Challenges and Rebuilding (1915-1945)

The First World War disrupted football, and United faced further challenges in the interwar years. Despite the legendary status of players like Charlie Roberts and Billy Meredith, the club struggled for consistency and was relegated to the Second Division in 1922. They bounced back and forth between the divisions, with financial difficulties continuing to cast a shadow.

World War II brought football to a halt once again. Old Trafford suffered significant damage from bombing raids, forcing the team to play its home matches at Manchester City's Maine Road ground.

The period between 1915 and 1945 was a turbulent one for Manchester United, marked by both on-field struggles and off-field challenges. Let's delve deeper into this era:

- The Impact of World War I: The First World War had a profound impact on the club. Many players enlisted to fight, disrupting the team's stability and progress.[1] Football leagues were suspended, and the club faced financial difficulties as revenue streams dried up.

- Post-War Struggles: After the war, Manchester United struggled to regain its pre-war form. The team lacked consistency and faced relegation to the Second Division in 1922. They yo-yoed between the divisions throughout the

1920s and 1930s, never quite managing to establish themselves as a dominant force.

- Financial Troubles: Financial difficulties continued to plague the club during this period. The Great Depression exacerbated these problems, and at one point, the club was on the brink of bankruptcy again. They relied on fundraising efforts and the generosity of benefactors to stay afloat.

- The Rise of Local Rivals: While Manchester United struggled, their local rivals, Manchester City, enjoyed a period of success, winning the FA Cup in 1934 and the league title in 1937. This added to the frustration of United fans and intensified the rivalry between the two clubs.

- World War II and the Bombing of Old Trafford: The outbreak of World War II brought further disruption. Football was once again suspended, and Old Trafford suffered significant damage from German bombing raids in 1941. The club was forced to play its home matches at Manchester City's Maine Road ground.

- Key Figures: Despite the challenges, there were some bright spots during this period. John Chapman managed the club for a significant portion of this era, guiding them through difficult times. Players like Jack Rowley and Joe Spence provided moments of brilliance on the pitch.

- A Glimmer of Hope: Towards the end of the war, there were signs of recovery. United reached the FA Cup final in 1944, losing to Charlton Athletic. This performance offered a glimmer of hope for the future.

A Club on the Brink:

By 1945, Manchester United was a club that had endured significant challenges. The war had taken its toll, both physically and financially. Old Trafford lay in ruins, and the team had struggled for consistency on the pitch. However, the club's spirit remained unbroken, and the stage was set for a new era of success.

The Busby Era and the Munich Tragedy (1945-1969)

The appointment of Matt Busby as manager in 1945 marked the beginning of a new era. Busby, a young and innovative coach, implemented a youth-focused policy that would become a hallmark of the club. He nurtured a generation of talented young players, known as the "Busby Babes," who won the league title in 1952, 1956, and 1957.

Tragedy struck in 1958 when the team's plane crashed in Munich, killing eight players and injuring many others. Busby himself was critically injured but survived. The Munich Air Disaster devastated the club and the city of Manchester.

Despite the immense loss, Busby rebuilt the team, and with the emergence of stars like Bobby Charlton and George Best, United won the FA Cup in 1963 and the league title in 1965 and 1967. The pinnacle of Busby's reign came in 1968 when Manchester United became the first English club to win the European Cup, defeating Benfica in the final at Wembley.

The appointment of Matt Busby as manager in 1945 ushered in a golden age for Manchester United. However, this period was also marked by unimaginable tragedy. Here's a closer look:

The Visionary Leader:

- Matt Busby's Philosophy: Busby was a young and forward-thinking manager with a clear vision for the club. He prioritized youth development, implemented a new training regime, and instilled an attacking style of play. He had a keen eye for talent and wasn't afraid to give young players a chance.

The Busby Babes:

- A New Generation: Busby assembled a squad of talented young players, many of whom had come through the club's youth system. This group, known as the "Busby Babes," became synonymous with exciting, attacking football. They were a symbol of hope and renewal in post-war Britain.

- Early Dominance: The Busby Babes quickly made their mark, winning the FA Cup in 1948 and finishing as league runners-up in three consecutive seasons. They then clinched the league title in 1952, signaling their arrival as a dominant force. Further league titles followed in 1956 and 1957.

European Adventures:

- Pioneers in Europe: In 1956, Manchester United became one of the first English teams to compete in the European Cup, despite opposition from the Football League. Their participation marked the beginning of a long and successful association with European competition.

The Munich Air Disaster:

- February 6, 1958: Tragedy struck on the return journey from a European Cup tie in Belgrade. The team's plane crashed in Munich after a refueling stop, killing 23 people, including eight players: Geoff Bent, Roger Byrne, Eddie Colman, Duncan Edwards, Mark Jones, David Pegg, Tommy Taylor, and Billy Whelan.

- A Devastated City and Club: The Munich Air Disaster sent shockwaves through Manchester and the world of football. Busby himself was critically injured and spent months in hospital. The loss of so many young lives was a devastating blow to the club and the city.

Rebuilding and Resilience:

- Jimmy Murphy's Leadership: With Busby recovering, assistant manager Jimmy Murphy took charge and guided the team to the FA Cup final that year, which they lost to Bolton

Wanderers. He played a crucial role in keeping the club going in the aftermath of the tragedy.

- A New Generation Emerges: Busby gradually rebuilt the team, blending experienced players with promising youngsters. Bobby Charlton, one of the survivors of Munich, became a key figure, alongside new signings like Denis Law and Pat Crerand.

- Triumphant Return: In 1963, Manchester United won the FA Cup, a symbolic victory that demonstrated the club's resilience. They went on to win the league title in 1965 and 1967.

European Glory:

- Conquering Europe: In 1968, ten years after Munich, Manchester United achieved the ultimate triumph by winning the European Cup, defeating Benfica 4-1 in the final at Wembley. This victory was a testament to Busby's leadership and the indomitable spirit of the club.

A Lasting Legacy:

The Busby era is a defining period in Manchester United's history. Busby's influence on the club's philosophy, his emphasis on youth development, and his ability to rebuild after tragedy have left a lasting legacy. The Munich Air Disaster remains a poignant reminder of the fragility of life, but it also highlights the enduring strength and resilience of the human spirit.

Conclusion

Manchester United's history is a tapestry of triumphs and tragedies, of financial struggles and periods of dominance. From its humble beginnings as a railway workers' team to its status as a global footballing giant, the club has endured and overcome numerous challenges. The early successes, the rebuilding efforts after the wars, and the triumphs under Matt Busby laid the foundation for the modern-day Manchester United, a club that continues to inspire millions around the world.

Manchester United's journey from a humble railway workers' team to a global footballing powerhouse is a testament to the enduring power of resilience, ambition, and the human spirit. The club's history is etched in both triumph and tragedy, a story that resonates with fans worldwide.

The early successes of Newton Heath, the transformation into Manchester United, and the dominance under Matt Busby laid the foundation for the modern-day club. These periods showcased the club's ability to overcome challenges, adapt to changing circumstances, and consistently strive for excellence.

The Munich Air Disaster, a defining moment in the club's history, revealed the depths of its character. The tragedy, while devastating, ultimately brought the club and its supporters closer together, forging an unbreakable bond. The subsequent rebuilding efforts and the eventual triumph in the European Cup demonstrated the unwavering spirit and determination that lie at the heart of Manchester United.

Beyond the trophies and accolades, Manchester United's legacy extends to its impact on the global football landscape. The club's commitment to attacking football, its emphasis on youth development, and its ability to connect with fans across cultures and continents have made it a true icon of the sport.

Manchester United's story is not just about football; it's about the people who have shaped the club over the years – the players, managers, staff, and, most importantly, the fans. Their collective passion, loyalty, and unwavering support have been instrumental in the club's success and have helped to create a global community united by a shared love for the Red Devils.

As Manchester United continues to evolve and face new challenges, the values and traditions established throughout its rich history will continue to guide its path. The club's legacy serves as an inspiration, a reminder that even in the face of adversity, with courage, determination, and a belief in the power of collective spirit, anything is possible.

Chapter 2: Development and Legacy

Manchester United's history can be divided into several key phases, each marked by distinct characteristics and achievements:

1. The Early Years (1878-1945): From Railway Workers to Wartime Struggles

- Foundation and Early Successes: Founded as Newton Heath LYR Football Club in 1878, the club faced early financial struggles before finding its feet as Manchester United in the early 1900s, winning its first league titles and FA Cup
- Challenges and Rebuilding: The two World Wars disrupted the club's progress, with Old Trafford suffering bomb damage in World War II. Despite these setbacks, the club showed resilience and a determination to rebuild

To truly understand Manchester United's rise, we need to delve deeper into the challenges and triumphs of its formative years. This period, spanning from the club's foundation to the end of World War II, saw the club evolve from a humble group of railway workers to a professional football club navigating a rapidly changing world.

2. Birth of a Football Club (1878-1892):

- Newton Heath LYR Football Club: Founded in 1878 by the carriage and wagon department of the Lancashire and Yorkshire Railway[1] depot in Newton Heath, the club's early years were characterized by camaraderie and local competition.
- Early Matches: They played friendly games against other railway departments and local businesses on a field near the railway depot.
- Growing Ambition: The club gradually became more organized, participating in local cup competitions and joining The Combination, a regional league, in 1888.

3. Entering the Football League and Financial Hardship (1892-1902):

- Turning Professional: In 1889, Newton Heath made the significant step of turning professional, allowing them to attract better players and compete at a higher level.
- The Football League: In 1892, they were elected to the newly formed Football League First Division, a testament to their growing ambition.
- Relegation and Instability: Life in the First Division proved

challenging, and relegation to the Second Division followed in 1894. The club yo-yoed between the divisions, struggling to maintain stability.

- Financial Troubles: Financial difficulties were a constant concern, with the club relying on the support of the railway company and fundraising efforts.
- Bank Street Ground: In 1893, they moved to a new ground on Bank Street in Clayton, but the location next to a chemical works made for difficult playing conditions.

4. A New Beginning as Manchester United (1902-1914):

- On the Brink of Collapse: By 1902, Newton Heath was on the verge of bankruptcy.
- John Henry Davies to the Rescue: Local brewer John Henry Davies, along with four other businessmen, invested in the club, saving it from financial ruin.
- Manchester United is Born: On April 24, 1902, the club was renamed Manchester United, marking a fresh start.
- Early Successes: Under the management of Ernest Mangnall, United won its first FA Cup in 1909 and its first league titles in 1908 and 1911.

- Old Trafford: In 1910, the club moved to its now-famous home, Old Trafford, a symbol of its growing ambition.

5. Wartime Challenges and Interwar Years (1914-1945):

- World War I Disruption: The First World War brought football to a halt, with many players enlisting in the armed forces. The club faced renewed financial challenges.
- Interwar Struggles: Despite the presence of legendary players like Charlie Roberts and Billy Meredith, the club struggled for consistency in the interwar years.
- Relegation and Financial Woes: They were relegated to the Second Division again in 1922 and continued to face financial difficulties.
- World War II and Bombing of Old Trafford: The Second World War brought further disruption. Old Trafford was damaged by bombing raids, forcing the team to play at Manchester City's Maine Road.

6. Key Takeaways from the Early Years:

- Resilience and Determination: Despite facing numerous challenges, including financial difficulties, relegations, and the disruption of two World Wars, the club showed a remarkable ability to persevere and rebuild.

- Foundation for Future Success: The early years were crucial in establishing the club's identity and laying the groundwork for future success. The move to Old Trafford, the early triumphs, and the development of a strong fanbase all contributed to the club's growth.

- A Club Forged in adversity: The early years instilled a fighting spirit and a determination to overcome challenges, qualities that would define Manchester United throughout its history.

7. The Busby Babes and Munich (1945-1969): A Golden Era and Unthinkable Tragedy

- Matt Busby's Vision: The arrival of Matt Busby as manager in 1945 marked a turning point. His focus on youth development led to the emergence of the "Busby Babes," a talented young team that won league titles and captivated fans with their attacking style.

- The Munich Air Disaster (1958): The tragic plane crash in Munich claimed the lives of eight players and cast a long shadow over the club. Busby himself was seriously injured.

- Rebuilding and European Glory: Despite the immense loss, Busby rebuilt the team, culminating in the European Cup triumph in 1968, a testament to the club's resilience and spirit.

8. The Post-Busby Years (1969-1986): A Period of Transition and Decline

- Struggles for Consistency: Following Busby's retirement, the club struggled to maintain its dominance. A series of managerial changes and a lack of on-field success led to a period of relative decline.
- Relegation and FA Cup Success: United were relegated to the Second Division in 1974 but bounced back immediately. They won the FA Cup in 1977, offering a glimmer of hope during a challenging period.

9. The Sir Alex Ferguson Era (1986-2013): Dominance and Dynasty

- Building a Winning Culture: The arrival of Sir Alex Ferguson in 1986 ushered in an era of unprecedented success. Ferguson instilled a winning mentality, developed young talent, and established a culture of dominance.

- Premier League Dominance: United became the dominant force in the newly formed Premier League, winning 13 titles under Ferguson. They also won five FA Cups and four League Cups.
- The Treble (1999): The pinnacle of Ferguson's reign came in 1999 when United achieved a historic treble, winning the Premier League, FA Cup, and Champions League.
- European Success: In addition to the 1999 Champions League title, United reached three other finals under Ferguson, cementing their status as a European powerhouse.

10. Post-Ferguson and Rebuilding (2013-Present): A New Chapter

- Challenges of Transition: Ferguson's retirement in 2013 marked the end of an era. The club has since faced challenges in replicating his success, with a series of managerial changes and inconsistent performances.
- Modern-Day Rebuilding: Despite the challenges, there have been signs of progress in recent years. The club has invested heavily in new players and is working to rebuild a squad capable of challenging for major honors once again.

11. Manchester United's Global Influence:

- A Global Brand: Manchester United has become one of the most recognizable and supported football clubs in the world. Its global fanbase, commercial success, and influence on the sport are undeniable.

- Youth Development: The club's commitment to youth development has produced generations of talented players, many of whom have gone on to achieve success at the highest level.

- A Symbol of Resilience: Manchester United's history, marked by both triumph and tragedy, has made it a symbol of resilience and the enduring power of the human spirit.

Manchester United's story is far from over. The club continues to evolve, facing new challenges and striving for success in a rapidly changing football landscape. Its rich history, however, provides a strong foundation and a source of inspiration as it embarks on this new chapter.

Part 3: Global Fanbase

Manchester United's global reach is a testament to its rich history, iconic status, and strategic efforts to engage with fans worldwide. With an estimated fan base exceeding 1.1 billion, the club's influence extends far beyond the confines of Old Trafford, impacting cultures and communities across continents.

A Global Fan Base:

- Continental Spread: Manchester United's supporters are spread across the globe, with significant followings in Asia (particularly in China, India, and Southeast Asia), North America, Africa, and Europe (beyond the UK). This widespread support is a result of various factors, including the club's historic achievements, its association with legendary players, and its proactive engagement with international fans.

Cultural Impact:

- Asia: In many Asian countries, Manchester United has become a symbol of aspiration and success. The club's popularity has led to the establishment of numerous fan clubs, the growth of youth academies, and the organization of local tournaments. United's pre-season tours in Asia have further strengthened its connection with fans in the region.

- North America: Manchester United's presence in North America has grown significantly in recent years, fueled by the increasing popularity of the Premier League. The club's matches are widely televised, and its merchandise is readily available. United's pre-season tours in the US and Canada have attracted large crowds and generated significant media attention.

- Europe: Beyond its loyal fanbase in the UK, Manchester United enjoys widespread support across Europe. The club's historic rivalries with teams like Real Madrid, Barcelona, and Bayern Munich have captivated fans for generations. United's success in European competitions has further solidified its status as a continental powerhouse.

Fan Engagement Strategies:

- Pre-Season Tours: Manchester United regularly embarks on pre-season tours to different continents, allowing fans around the world to experience the club firsthand. These tours provide opportunities for fans to watch matches, meet players, and participate in various events.

- Social Media Campaigns: The club actively engages with fans through various social media platforms, including Facebook, Twitter, and Instagram. These platforms provide a direct channel for communication, allowing fans to stay updated on club news, interact with players, and participate in online discussions.

- Fan Clubs: Manchester United has a vast network of official fan clubs around the world. These clubs provide a sense of community for supporters, organizing local events, screenings of matches, and trips to Old Trafford. They play a crucial role in fostering a sense of belonging and loyalty among fans.

- Digital Content: The club produces a wide range of digital content, including videos, articles, and interactive features, tailored to different audiences and languages. This content helps to keep fans engaged and informed, regardless of their location.

Manchester United's global reach is a testament to its ability to transcend geographical boundaries and connect with people through the shared passion for football. The club's cultural impact is evident in the diverse communities that have embraced it as their own.

Through strategic fan engagement initiatives, Manchester United continues to strengthen its bond with supporters worldwide, fostering a global community united by a love for the Red Devils.

Chapter 2: Famous Players of Manchester United FC Football

Part 1: The Legends

Manchester United Legends:

These players have not only achieved incredible success on the pitch but also embodied the spirit and values of Manchester United, leaving an indelible mark on the club's history and inspiring generations of fans.

1. George Best (1963-1974): The "Fifth Beatle"

- Early Career: Spotted by a Manchester United scout at the age of 15, Best's talent was evident from the start. He made his first-team debut at 17 and quickly became a sensation.
- Contributions: Best was a dazzling winger with exceptional dribbling skills, pace, and an eye for goal. He was a key figure in United's league title wins in 1965 and 1967 and the European Cup triumph in 1968.
- Major Achievements:
  - European Cup: 1968

- League Titles: 1965, 1967
- Ballon d'Or: 1968
- **Legacy:** Best's flamboyant style and off-field charisma made him a global icon. He is considered one of the most naturally gifted footballers of all time, and his impact on the game transcended sport.

The Belfast Boy:

- **Humble Beginnings:** Born in Belfast, Northern Ireland, Best's natural talent was evident from a young age. He honed his skills playing street football and quickly rose through the ranks of local youth teams.

Manchester United Beckons:

- **"A Genius":** At 15, Best was spotted by Manchester United scout Bob Bishop, who famously telegrammed Matt Busby: "I think I've found you a genius."
- **First Team Debut:** Best made his first-team debut at 17 and quickly became a sensation, captivating fans with his dazzling dribbling skills, incredible balance, and audacious goals.

The "Fifth Beatle":

- Pop Culture Icon: Best's good looks, long hair, and rebellious attitude captured the spirit of the 1960s. He became a pop culture icon, dubbed the "Fifth Beatle" by the press.
- Media Frenzy: His fame transcended the world of football, with his every move followed by the paparazzi. He embraced the celebrity lifestyle, frequenting nightclubs and enjoying the trappings of his success.

On the Pitch:

- Unstoppable Winger: Best was a nightmare for defenders. His ability to beat players with ease, combined with his clinical finishing, made him one of the most exciting players to watch.
- European Cup Triumph: Best played a pivotal role in Manchester United's European Cup victory in 1968, scoring a memorable goal in the final against Benfica.

The Downward Spiral:

- Struggles with Fame: Best's off-field lifestyle began to affect his career. His struggles with alcoholism and personal problems led to conflicts with the club and ultimately contributed to his departure from Manchester United in 1974 at the age of 27.

- Later Career: He continued to play for various clubs around the world but never reached the same heights.

A Complex Legacy:

- Football Genius: Best is widely regarded as one of the most naturally gifted footballers of all time. His skill, flair, and impact on the game are undeniable.
- Troubled Icon: His struggles with fame and addiction serve as a cautionary tale, but they also humanize the legend, reminding us that even the most talented individuals are not immune to personal demons.
- Enduring Inspiration: Despite his flaws, Best remains an inspiration to many. His story is a testament to the power of talent, the allure of fame, and the complexities of human nature.

2. Sir Bobby Charlton (1956-1973): The "Knight of the Busby Babes"

- Early Career: A survivor of the Munich Air Disaster, Charlton emerged as a leader and a symbol of resilience for the club.
- Contributions: Charlton was a prolific goalscorer and a creative force in midfield. He was instrumental in United's rebuilding efforts after Munich and played a key role in their league title wins in 1965 and 1967, as well as the European Cup victory in 1968.
- Major Achievements:
  - World Cup: 1966 (with England)
  - European Cup: 1968
  - League Titles: 1957, 1965, 1967
  - Ballon d'Or: 1966
- Legacy: Charlton is Manchester United's all-time leading goalscorer and a true legend of the game. His dedication, loyalty, and sportsmanship have made him an ambassador for the club and a role model for generations of players.

Sir Bobby Charlton (1956-1973): The "Knight of the Busby Babes" - Embodiment of Courage and Resilience

The Ashington Prodigy:

- Footballing Family: Born into a footballing family in Ashington, Northumberland, Charlton's talent was evident from a young age. He followed in the footsteps of his uncles, Jackie Milburn and Jack Charlton, both of whom played professional football.
- Joining the Busby Babes: Charlton joined Manchester United's youth system in 1953 and quickly progressed to the first team, becoming part of the legendary "Busby Babes."

Surviving Munich:

- A Day of Tragedy: On February 6, 1958, Charlton was involved in the Munich Air Disaster, which claimed the lives of eight of his teammates and left him with injuries. This tragedy deeply affected him, but it also fueled his determination to honor the memory of those lost.
- A Symbol of Hope: Charlton's survival and subsequent return to the pitch made him a symbol of hope and resilience for the club and its fans.

The Heart of a Champion:

- Attacking Midfielder: Charlton was a versatile and dynamic attacking midfielder with exceptional passing range, vision, and a thunderous shot. He was also a prolific goalscorer, finding the net with remarkable consistency.

- Leading the Rebuilding: He played a pivotal role in United's rebuilding efforts after Munich, helping the club win the FA Cup in 1963 and league titles in 1965 and 1967.
- European Glory: In 1968, Charlton captained Manchester United to their first European Cup triumph, scoring two goals in the final against Benfica.

International Success:

- World Cup Winner: Charlton was a key member of the England team that won the World Cup in 1966. He scored three goals in the tournament, including two in the semi-final against Portugal.

A True Gentleman:

- Humility and Sportsmanship: Charlton was known for his humility, sportsmanship, and dedication to the game. He was a true ambassador for Manchester United and for football in general.
- Knighted for Services to Football: In 1994, Charlton was knighted for his services to football, recognizing his

contributions both on and off the pitch.

A Legacy of Greatness:

- All-Time Leading Goalscorer: Charlton held the record for most goals scored for Manchester United (249) for over four decades until Wayne Rooney surpassed him in 2017.
- Club Ambassador: He remains a beloved figure at Old Trafford, serving as a club ambassador and representing Manchester United with dignity and grace.

3. Ryan Giggs (1991-2014): The "Welsh Wizard"

- Early Career: Giggs made his debut at 17 and quickly established himself as a key player in the Premier League era.
- Contributions: Giggs was a versatile winger known for his pace, dribbling skills, and crossing ability. He adapted his game over the years, becoming a more central player in his later career. He was a vital part of United's dominance under Sir Alex Ferguson.
- Major Achievements:
  - Premier League Titles: 13
  - Champions League: 2
  - FA Cup: 4
  - League Cup: 4
- Legacy: Giggs is the most decorated player in English football history and holds the record for most appearances for Manchester United. His longevity, consistency, and adaptability make him a true legend of the club.

4. Eric Cantona (1992-1997): "King Eric"

- Early Career: Cantona arrived from Leeds United and immediately transformed Manchester United's fortunes.

- Contributions: Cantona was a charismatic and enigmatic striker with exceptional skill and a powerful presence on the pitch. He was a catalyst for United's success in the Premier League era, inspiring his teammates and intimidating opponents.

- Major Achievements:
  - Premier League Titles: 4
  - FA Cup: 2

- Legacy: Cantona's impact on Manchester United extended beyond his on-field contributions. His confidence, swagger, and iconic moments, like his upturned collar celebration, made him a cult hero and a symbol of the club's resurgence.

A Nomadic Start:

- Early Career in France: Cantona's early career in France was marked by both brilliance and controversy. His talent was undeniable, but his fiery temperament often led to clashes with authorities and coaches.

- Brief Stint at Leeds: He had a brief but successful spell at

Leeds United, helping them win the league title in 1992 before making a controversial move to their rivals, Manchester United.

The King of Old Trafford:

- Instant Impact: Cantona's arrival at Old Trafford had an immediate impact. His presence, confidence, and undeniable skill galvanized the team, transforming them into title contenders.
- The "Collar Up" Era: Cantona exuded an aura of arrogance and self-belief, famously playing with his collar upturned. This, combined with his exceptional skill and crucial goals, made him a cult hero among United fans.
- Leadership and Inspiration: Cantona was more than just a goalscorer; he was a leader who inspired his teammates and instilled a winning mentality. He demanded the best from those around him and led by example.

A Controversial Genius:

- The Kung-Fu Incident: Cantona's time at United was not without controversy. In 1995, he was involved in an infamous incident where he launched a kung-fu kick at a Crystal Palace fan, resulting in a lengthy ban.

- Philosophical Reflections: Cantona's enigmatic personality was often on display in his interviews and public appearances. His philosophical musings and cryptic pronouncements added to his mystique.

A Lasting Impact:

- Premier League Dominance: Cantona played a crucial role in Manchester United's early Premier League success, helping them win four titles in five seasons.
- Cultural Icon: He became a cultural icon, transcending the world of football. His image adorned posters and magazine covers, and his pronouncements were often quoted in the media.
- Early Retirement: Cantona surprisingly retired from football at the age of 30, leaving a void at Old Trafford and in the hearts of fans.

"King Eric"

- A Catalyst for Change: Cantona's impact on Manchester United was profound. He was the catalyst for the club's dominance in the Premier League era, inspiring a generation of players and leaving an enduring legacy.
- Unique Charisma: His unique blend of skill, charisma, and

controversy made him a truly unforgettable figure in football history. He will forever be remembered as "King Eric," the enigmatic genius who helped to redefine Manchester United.

5. Paul Scholes (1994-2013): The "Ginger Prince"

- Early Career: Scholes came through the club's youth system and became a mainstay in midfield for almost two decades.
- Contributions: Scholes was a complete midfielder with exceptional passing range, vision, and a powerful shot. He was a key figure in United's dominance under Sir Alex Ferguson, dictating play from the center of the park.
- Major Achievements:
    - Premier League Titles: 11
    - Champions League: 2
    - FA Cup: 3
    - League Cup: 2
- Legacy: Scholes is widely regarded as one of the greatest midfielders of his generation. His intelligence, technique, and dedication to the club have made him a true legend of Manchester United.

From Salford to Stardom:

- A Local Lad: Born and raised in Salford, Greater Manchester, Scholes joined the Manchester United youth academy at the age of 14. He was part of a talented generation of young players known as "Fergie's Fledglings."

- Early Promise: Scholes progressed through the ranks, impressing with his passing range, vision, and goalscoring ability. He made his first-team debut in 1994 and quickly established himself as a key player.

The Complete Midfielder:

- Passing Master: Scholes was renowned for his pinpoint passing accuracy, both short and long. He could dictate the tempo of a game, create scoring opportunities, and unlock defenses with his vision.

- Goalscoring Threat: Despite his midfield role, Scholes possessed a powerful shot and a knack for scoring crucial goals. He often arrived late in the box to devastating effect.

- Tough Tackler: Scholes was not afraid to put in a tackle, and his competitive spirit and determination were evident in every game.

A Key Figure in United's Dominance:

- Premier League Era: Scholes was a vital part of Manchester United's success in the Premier League era. He formed a formidable midfield partnership with Roy Keane, providing the platform for the team's attacking flair.

- Champions League Glory: Scholes won two Champions League titles with United, in 1999 and 2008, showcasing his ability to perform on the biggest stage.

The "Silent Assassin":

- Quiet Leader: Scholes was a quiet and unassuming character, letting his football do the talking. He was a respected leader in the dressing room and a role model for younger players.
- Disciplinary Issues: Scholes was known for his aggressive tackling style, which occasionally landed him in trouble with referees. He holds the record for the most yellow cards in Premier League history.

Retirement and Comeback:

- Hanging Up His Boots: Scholes announced his retirement in 2011 but returned to the team in January 2012 after realizing he still had a contribution to make.
- Second Retirement: He finally retired for good in 2013, ending a remarkable career spanning nearly two decades.

A True Legend:

- One-Club Man: Scholes spent his entire professional career at

Manchester United, a testament to his loyalty and dedication to the club.

- Admired by Peers: He is widely regarded as one of the greatest midfielders of his generation, earning praise from fellow professionals and pundits alike.
- Enduring Legacy: Scholes' impact on Manchester United is immeasurable. His skill, vision, and commitment to the club have made him a true legend, and his name will forever be etched in the hearts of United fans worldwide.

These five legends, along with many others, have contributed to Manchester United's rich history and global appeal. Their achievements on the pitch, combined with their unique personalities and contributions to the club's culture, have secured their places in football folklore.

Chapter 2: Modern-Day Stars

Modern Manchester United Stars:

These players represent the modern era of Manchester United, showcasing exceptional talent, achieving significant milestones, and leaving their mark on the club's history.

1. Cristiano Ronaldo (2003-2009 & 2021-2023): The "Portuguese Magnifico"

- Early Career at United: Signed as a teenager from Sporting CP, Ronaldo quickly became a fan favorite with his dazzling skills, electrifying pace, and audacious goals. He developed into one of the world's best players during his first stint at Old Trafford.
- First Stint Highlights:
  - Premier League titles (3): 2006–07, 2007–08, 2008–09
  - Champions League: 2007-08
  - FA Cup: 2003-04
  - Ballon d'Or: 2008
  - FIFA World Player of the Year: 2008

- Memorable moments: His stunning free-kick against Portsmouth, his hat-trick against Newcastle United, and his Champions League final goal against Chelsea.
- Return to Old Trafford: In a sensational move, Ronaldo returned to Manchester United in 2021, bringing a wave of excitement and expectation.
- Second Stint Highlights:
  - Despite the team's struggles, Ronaldo continued to score goals, breaking the all-time record for most goals in men's international football.
  - Memorable moments: His brace against Newcastle on his second debut, his late goals against Villarreal and Atalanta in the Champions League.
- Departure: Ronaldo left the club in 2023 after a controversial interview.
- Legacy: Ronaldo's impact on Manchester United is undeniable. His dedication to his craft, his relentless pursuit of excellence, and his remarkable goalscoring record have cemented his place as a club legend, despite the controversial end to his second spell.

The Arrival of a Prodigy (2003-2009):

- Teenage Sensation: Signed from Sporting CP in 2003 at the age of 18, Ronaldo immediately caught the eye with his dazzling footwork, blistering pace, and audacious trickery.
- Early Development: While raw talent was evident, Sir Alex Ferguson nurtured Ronaldo, helping him channel his abilities and develop into a more complete player. He gradually transformed from a flashy winger to a lethal goalscorer.
- Rise to Superstardom: Ronaldo's performances for United saw him rise to global stardom. He won his first Ballon d'Or in 2008, marking his arrival as the world's best player.
- Memorable Moments:
  - The Free-kick Specialist: Ronaldo became renowned for his powerful and accurate free-kicks, often leaving goalkeepers helpless. His iconic free-kick against Portsmouth in 2008 is a prime example.
  - Champions League Heroics: He scored crucial goals in United's Champions League triumph in 2008, including a towering header in the final against Chelsea.
  - Step-overs and Flicks: Ronaldo's signature step-overs and flicks became a trademark of his early years,

showcasing his incredible skill and flair.

The Homecoming (2021-2023):

- A Sensational Return: In the summer of 2021, Ronaldo made a sensational return to Old Trafford, sending shockwaves through the football world. His arrival brought a renewed sense of excitement and expectation to the club.
- Goalscoring Prowess: Despite being in the latter stages of his career, Ronaldo continued to score goals at an impressive rate, proving that he still had the ability to perform at the highest level.
- Leadership and Mentorship: Ronaldo's presence in the dressing room provided a boost for the younger players, who looked up to him as a role model and leader.
- Memorable Moments:
  - The Second Debut: Ronaldo marked his return with a brace against Newcastle United, reminding everyone of his goalscoring prowess.
  - Champions League Rescues: He scored crucial late goals in the Champions League against Villarreal and Atalanta, showcasing his ability to deliver in big moments.

- A Controversial Departure: Ronaldo's second stint at United ended in controversial circumstances in 2023. An explosive interview led to his contract being terminated.

The Ronaldo Legacy:

- A Global Icon: Ronaldo's impact on Manchester United transcends his goalscoring records and trophies. He is a global icon who has inspired millions with his dedication, work ethic, and relentless pursuit of greatness.
- A Complex Figure: Despite his undeniable talent and achievements, Ronaldo's time at United was also marked by moments of controversy and frustration. His departure left a mixed legacy, but his impact on the club's history is undeniable.
- The "Portuguese Magnifico": Ronaldo will forever be remembered as the "Portuguese Magnifico" who graced Old Trafford with his brilliance. His two spells at the club, though different in nature, both contributed to his legendary status and cemented his place in the hearts of Manchester United fans worldwide.

2. Wayne Rooney (2004-2017): The "White Pele"

- Early Promise: Rooney burst onto the scene as a teenager at Everton before joining Manchester United in 2004 for a then-record fee for a teenager. He quickly lived up to the hype, scoring a hat-trick on his Champions League debut.
- Record-Breaking Goalscorer: Rooney surpassed Sir Bobby Charlton to become Manchester United's all-time leading goalscorer with 253 goals in all competitions.
- Captain Fantastic: He captained the club for several years, leading by example with his passion, commitment, and tireless work ethic.
- Achievements:
  - Premier League titles (5): 2006–07, 2007–08, 2008–09, 2010–11, 2012–13
  - Champions League: 2007-08
  - FA Cup: 2015-16
  - League Cup (3): 2005-06, 2009-10, 2016-17
  - Memorable moments: His overhead kick against Manchester City, his last-minute winner against AC Milan, and his record-breaking goal against Stoke City.
- Legacy: Rooney's impact on Manchester United is immense.

He is not only the club's record goalscorer but also a symbol of its fighting spirit and determination. He is considered one of the greatest English footballers of all time.

The Boy Wonder:

- Everton Roots: Born and raised in Croxteth, Liverpool, Rooney's footballing journey began at Everton. He joined their youth academy at the age of 9 and burst onto the scene as a teenager, scoring a spectacular goal against Arsenal at the age of 16.
- "Remember the Name": Rooney's precocious talent and fearless attitude quickly made him one of the most sought-after young players in the world. His performance for England at Euro 2004 cemented his status as a rising star.

A Record-Breaking Red Devil:

- Arrival at Old Trafford: In 2004, Rooney joined Manchester United for a then-record fee for a teenager. He immediately lived up to the hype, scoring a hat-trick on his Champions League debut against Fenerbahçe.
- Goalscoring Machine: Rooney's goalscoring record for United is simply phenomenal. He surpassed Sir Bobby Charlton's long-standing record to become the club's all-time

leading scorer with 253 goals in all competitions.

- Adaptability and Versatility: While primarily a striker, Rooney's versatility allowed him to play in various positions, including attacking midfield and even deeper midfield roles. This adaptability made him an invaluable asset to the team throughout his career.

Captain Fantastic:

- Leading by Example: Rooney was appointed captain of Manchester United in 2014, a testament to his leadership qualities and influence within the squad. He led by example with his passion, commitment, and never-say-die attitude.
- Inspiring Teammates: Rooney's presence on the pitch inspired his teammates to raise their game. He was a vocal leader, demanding the best from those around him and driving the team forward.

Memorable Moments:

- The Overhead Kick: Rooney's spectacular overhead kick against Manchester City in 2011 is considered one of the greatest goals in Premier League history. It was a moment of pure brilliance that showcased his athleticism and technical ability.

- Last-Minute Winners: Rooney had a knack for scoring crucial goals, often in the dying moments of matches. His last-minute winner against AC Milan in the Champions League in 2010 is a prime example.
- Breaking the Record: Rooney's record-breaking goal against Stoke City in 2017 was a fitting tribute to his remarkable career at Manchester United.

The Rooney Legacy:

- A True Legend: Rooney's impact on Manchester United goes far beyond his goalscoring record. He was a talismanic figure who embodied the club's fighting spirit and winning mentality.
- A Symbol of Dedication: His dedication to the club, his willingness to adapt his game, and his unwavering commitment to excellence make him a true role model for young players.
- The "White Pele": Wayne Rooney, the "White Pele," will forever be remembered as one of the greatest players to ever wear the Manchester United shirt. His name is etched in the club's history, and his legacy will inspire generations to come.

3. Marcus Rashford (2015-present): The "Mancunian Hero"

- Academy Graduate: Rashford rose through the ranks of Manchester United's academy and burst onto the scene with two goals on his first-team debut in 2016.
- On-Field Prowess: Rashford is a dynamic forward with blistering pace, skillful dribbling, and a clinical finish. He has consistently been one of United's top performers in recent years.
- Off-Field Activism: Rashford has become a powerful voice for social change, campaigning against child poverty and food insecurity in the UK. He has used his platform to raise awareness and effect real change, earning widespread praise and recognition.
- Achievements:
  - FA Cup: 2015-16
  - League Cup: 2016-17
  - UEFA Europa League: 2016-17
  - Memorable moments: His brace on his debut against Midtjylland, his free-kick against Chelsea, and his crucial goals in the Europa League campaign.

- Legacy: Rashford represents the modern-day Manchester United player – talented, committed, and socially conscious. He is an inspiration to young people both on and off the pitch, and his impact on the club and society is significant.

These three players, along with many other talented individuals, have contributed to Manchester United's continued success and global appeal in the modern era. Their achievements, memorable moments, and contributions to the club's legacy ensure that they will be remembered as some of the greatest players to wear the famous red shirt.

Chapter 3: Key Achievements

Manchester United: Individual and Team Achievements

Here's a glimpse into the remarkable achievements of Manchester United players, both individually and as a team, showcasing their contributions to the club's rich history:

Individual Achievements:

- Ballon d'Or Winners:

  - George Best (1968)

  - Bobby Charlton (1966)

  - Denis Law (1964)

  - Cristiano Ronaldo (2008)

- Premier League Golden Boot Winners:

  - Cristiano Ronaldo (2007-08)

  - Dimitar Berbatov (2010-11, shared)

  - Robin van Persie (2012-13)

- European Golden Shoe Winners:

  - Cristiano Ronaldo (2007-08)

- PFA Players' Player of the Year:

  - Mark Hughes (1988-89, 1990-91)

  - Eric Cantona (1993-94)

  - Roy Keane (1999-2000)

  - Ruud van Nistelrooy (2001-02)

  - Cristiano Ronaldo (2006-07, 2007-08)

  - Wayne Rooney (2009-10)

- FWA Footballer of the Year:

  - Bobby Charlton (1965-66)

  - George Best (1967-68)

  - Eric Cantona (1995-96)

  - Cristiano Ronaldo (2006-07, 2007-08)

  - Wayne Rooney (2009-10)

Team Achievements:

- League Titles (20): A record number of English top-flight titles, including 13 Premier League titles under Sir Alex Ferguson.

- FA Cup (12): One of the most successful clubs in the competition's history.

- League Cup (6): A consistent contender in the League Cup, with victories spread across different eras.
- Champions League (3): European champions in 1968, 1999, and 2008.
- UEFA Europa League (1): Victorious in 2017, completing the set of major European trophies.
- Intercontinental Cup (1): World champions in 1999 after winning the Champions League.
- FIFA Club World Cup (1): World champions in 2008.

Iconic Performances and Goals:

- George Best vs. Benfica (1968 European Cup Final): Best's mesmerizing performance and goal in the final helped United become the first English club to win the European Cup.
- Bobby Charlton vs. Benfica (1968 European Cup Final): Charlton scored two goals in the final, cementing his place as a United legend.
- Eric Cantona vs. Sunderland (1996): Cantona's iconic chip goal and "collar up" celebration epitomized his swagger and confidence.
- Ryan Giggs vs. Arsenal (1999 FA Cup Semi-Final): Giggs's stunning solo goal in extra time is considered one of the

greatest FA Cup goals of all time.

- Paul Scholes vs. Barcelona (2008 Champions League Semi-Final): Scholes's thunderous long-range goal secured United's place in the final.

- Cristiano Ronaldo vs. Portsmouth (2008): Ronaldo's incredible free-kick against Portsmouth showcased his power and accuracy.

- Wayne Rooney vs. Manchester City (2011): Rooney's overhead kick against City is regarded as one of the greatest goals in Premier League history.

- Marcus Rashford vs. Midtjylland (2016): Rashford's brace on his debut announced his arrival as a future star.

These are just a few examples of the many individual and team achievements that have contributed to Manchester United's rich history and global appeal. The club's legacy of success, combined with the iconic performances of its players, continues to inspire generations of fans worldwide.

Part 3: Games

Chapter 1: True-False Questions

History

1. True or False: Manchester United was originally founded as Newton Heath LYR Football Club.

   - True. The club was founded in 1878 by railway workers.

2. True or False: Manchester United has won the FA Cup more times than any other club.

   - False. Arsenal holds the record with 14 wins, while Manchester United has 12.

3. True or False: Manchester United's home ground, Old Trafford, was bombed during World War II.

   - True. The stadium suffered significant damage and required extensive repairs.

4. True or False: Matt Busby was the manager who led Manchester United to their first European Cup victory.

o   True. Busby guided the team to victory in 1968.

5. True or False: Manchester United were relegated to the Second Division in the 1970s.

    o   True. They were relegated in 1974 but bounced back to the First Division the following season.

6. True or False: Sir Alex Ferguson was the manager of Manchester United for over 25 years.

    o   True. Ferguson managed the club from 1986 to 2013.

7. True or False: Manchester United won the treble (Premier League, FA Cup, and Champions League) in 1998.

    o   False. They achieved the treble in 1999.

8. True or False: The Glazer family owns Manchester United.

    o   True. The Glazers acquired the club in 2005.

9. True or False: Manchester United has never won the FIFA Club World Cup.

    o   False. They won the tournament in 2008.

10. True or False: Manchester United played their home games at

Maine Road during World War II.

- ○ True. Old Trafford was damaged during the war, so they shared Manchester City's ground.

Famous Players

11. True or False: George Best was known as the "Fifth Beatle."

- ○ True. His fame and popularity in the 1960s earned him this nickname.

12. True or False: Bobby Charlton is Manchester United's all-time leading goalscorer.

- ○ False. Wayne Rooney surpassed Charlton's record in 2017.

13. True or False: Ryan Giggs played for Manchester United for over 20 years.

- ○ True. Giggs made his debut in 1991 and retired in 2014.

14. True or False: Eric Cantona was known for his calm and reserved demeanor.

- False. Cantona was known for his fiery temperament and controversial moments.

15. True or False: Paul Scholes spent his entire professional career at Manchester United.

  - True. Scholes is a one-club man.

16. True or False: Cristiano Ronaldo won the Ballon d'Or while playing for Manchester United.

  - True. He won the award in 2008.

17. True or False: Wayne Rooney is the only player to score over 200 goals for Manchester United.

  - False. Bobby Charlton also achieved this feat.

18. True or False: Marcus Rashford is a product of Manchester United's youth academy.

  - True. Rashford came through the ranks at United.

19. True or False: David Beckham started his career at Manchester United.

  - True. Beckham was a product of United's youth

system.

20. True or False: Peter Schmeichel was a goalkeeper for Manchester United.

   ○ True. Schmeichel was a legendary goalkeeper for the club in the 1990s.

Iconic Moments

21. True or False: Manchester United won the treble in the 1998-1999 season.

   ○ True. They won the Premier League, FA Cup, and Champions League.

22. True or False: Ole Gunnar Solskjaer scored the winning goal in the 1999 Champions League final.

   ○ True. His last-minute goal secured the victory against Bayern Munich.

23. True or False: The Munich Air Disaster occurred in 1958.

   ○ True. The plane crash claimed the lives of eight Manchester United players.

24. True or False: Eric Cantona's kung-fu kick incident occurred in 1995.

   ○ True. Cantona was banned for eight months for the incident.

25. True or False: Wayne Rooney scored an overhead kick against Liverpool.

   ○ False. His iconic overhead kick was against Manchester City.

26. True or False: Ryan Giggs scored a memorable solo goal against Arsenal in the 1999 FA Cup semi-final.

   ○ True. It is considered one of the greatest FA Cup goals ever.

27. True or False: Manchester United beat Chelsea in the 2008 Champions League final.

   ○ True. The match went to penalties after a 1-1 draw.

28. True or False: Cristiano Ronaldo scored a hat-trick on his Manchester United debut.

   ○ False. He scored a hat-trick against Newcastle in

2008.

29. True or False: David Beckham was known for his free-kick taking ability.

   ○ True. Beckham was a renowned free-kick specialist.

30. True or False: Roy Keane was a calm and composed captain.

   ○ False. Keane was known for his fiery temperament and leadership qualities.

Old Trafford

31. True or False: Old Trafford is the largest football stadium in England.

   ○ False. Wembley Stadium is the largest.

32. True or False: Old Trafford is known as the "Theatre of Dreams."

   ○ True. This nickname was given by Sir Bobby Charlton.

33. True or False: The Stretford End is a stand at Old Trafford.

- True. It is traditionally where the most vocal United fans gather.

34. True or False: The Munich Tunnel is a memorial at Old Trafford.

- True. It commemorates the victims of the Munich Air Disaster.

35. True or False: Old Trafford has hosted the Champions League final.

- True. It hosted the final in 2003.

36. True or False: The statue of the United Trinity outside Old Trafford features Best, Charlton, and Law.

- True. The statue commemorates these three legendary players.

37. True or False: Old Trafford has a capacity of over 80,000.

- False. The current capacity is around 74,000.

38. True or False: Manchester United have played at Old Trafford since 1910.

- True. The stadium has been their home ground for

over a century.

39. True or False: Old Trafford has hosted rugby league matches.

   o   True. It has hosted several major rugby league games.

40. True or False: Concerts have been held at Old Trafford.

   o   True. The stadium has hosted concerts by various

   artists, including Bruce Springsteen and Madonna.

Managers

41. True or False: Sir Matt Busby managed Manchester United in

   the 1940s and 1950s.

   o   True. He managed the club from 1945 to 1969, and

   again briefly in 1970-71.

42. True or False: Tommy Docherty managed Manchester United

   in the 1970s.

   o   True. He managed the club from 1972 to 1977.

43. True or False: Ron Atkinson managed Manchester United in

   the 1980s.

○ True. He managed the club from 1981 to 1986.

44. True or False: Sir Alex Ferguson managed Manchester United from 1986 to 2013.

○ True. His tenure is the longest in the club's history.

45. True or False: David Moyes was the immediate successor to Sir Alex Ferguson.

○ True. Moyes managed the club in the 2013-14 season.

46. True or False: Louis van Gaal led Manchester United to an FA Cup victory.

○ True. United won the FA Cup in 2016 under Van Gaal.

47. True or False: José Mourinho managed Manchester United for three seasons.

○ False. He managed the club for two and a half seasons.

48. True or False: Ole Gunnar Solskjær was a caretaker manager before being appointed permanently.

○ True. He took over as caretaker in 2018 and was

appointed permanently in 2019.

49. True or False: Ralf Rangnick was appointed interim manager after Ole Gunnar Solskjær's departure.

    ○ True. Rangnick took over in 2021.

50. True or False: Erik ten Hag is the current manager of Manchester United.

    ○ True. Ten Hag was appointed in 2022.

Club Culture & Identity

51. True or False: Manchester United's nickname is the Red Devils.

    ○ True. The nickname was adopted in the 1960s.

52. True or False: The club's traditional colours are red, white, and black.

    ○ True. These colours are reflected in their home kit.

53. True or False: "Glory Glory Man United" is a popular chant among the club's supporters.

- o True. It is one of the most well-known chants associated with the club.

54. True or False: The club has a strong tradition of youth development.

- o True. The "Busby Babes" and "Fergie's Fledglings" are examples of successful youth development.

55. True or False: Manchester United has a large global fan base.

- o True. The club is estimated to have over 1.1 billion fans worldwide.

56. True or False: The club has a rivalry with Liverpool FC.

- o True. This is one of the biggest rivalries in English football.

57. True or False: Manchester United has a museum at Old Trafford.

- o True. The museum showcases the club's history and achievements.

58. True or False: The club has a dedicated TV channel called MUTV.

○ True. MUTV provides behind-the-scenes access and exclusive content.

59. True or False: Manchester United women's team was formed in 2018.

○ True. The team has been competing in the Women's Super League.

60. True or False: Manchester United has a strong commitment to social responsibility.

○ True. The club is involved in various community initiatives and charitable activities.

Premier League Era

61. True or False: Manchester United won the first-ever Premier League title.

○ False. The first Premier League title was won by Manchester City in the 1992-93 season.

62. True or False: Eric Cantona played a key role in Manchester United's early Premier League success.

- True. Cantona helped United win four titles in the 1990s.

63. True or False: Manchester United have won the Premier League title more times than any other club.

- True. They have won 13 Premier League titles.

64. True or False: Ryan Giggs holds the record for most Premier League appearances.

- True. Giggs made 632 Premier League appearances.

65. True or False: Alan Shearer is the Premier League's all-time leading goalscorer.

- True. Shearer scored 260 Premier League goals.

66. True or False: The Premier League was formed in 1992.

- True. It replaced the First Division as the top tier of English football.

67. True or False: Manchester United have never been relegated from the Premier League.

- True. They have been a constant presence in the top flight.

68. True or False: Old Trafford has hosted Premier League matches since the league's inception.

  ○ True. Old Trafford has been a Premier League ground since 1992.

69. True or False: The Premier League is broadcast in over 200 countries.

  ○ True. It is one of the most-watched sports leagues in the world.

70. True or False: The Premier League is the most financially lucrative football league in the world.

  ○ True. It generates significant revenue from broadcasting rights and sponsorships.

European Competitions

71. True or False: Manchester United have won the European Cup/Champions League three times.

  ○ True. They won in 1968, 1999, and 2008.

72. True or False: Manchester United have reached the

Champions League final more times than any other English club.

- ○ False. Liverpool has reached the final more times.
73. True or False: Manchester United won the UEFA Cup Winners' Cup in 1991.

- ○ True. They beat Barcelona in the final.
74. True or False: Manchester United have never won the UEFA Europa League.

- ○ False. They won the Europa League in 2017.
75. True or False: Manchester United have played in the UEFA Cup/Europa League on several occasions.

- ○ True. They have participated in the competition throughout their history.
76. True or False: The European Cup was renamed the Champions League in 1992.

- ○ True. The rebranding marked a new era for the competition.
77. True or False: The Champions League final is always played

at a neutral venue.

- o True. The final is hosted by different cities each year.
78. True or False: The away goals rule is still used in European competitions.

- o False. The away goals rule was abolished in 2021.
79. True or False: VAR (Video Assistant Referee) is used in Champions League matches.

- o True. VAR was introduced to the Champions League in 2019.
80. True or False: The UEFA Super Cup is contested between the winners of the Champions League and the Europa League.

- o True. This annual match is a curtain-raiser for the European season.

Miscellaneous

81. True or False: The Busby Babes were a group of young Manchester United players in the 1950s.

- ○ True. They were known for their attacking style and youthful energy.
82. True or False: Fergie Time refers to the tendency for Manchester United to score late goals under Sir Alex Ferguson.

- ○ True. United were known for their late comebacks and dramatic finishes.
83. True or False: The Class of '92 refers to a group of young Manchester United players who emerged in the 1990s.

- ○ True. This group included Beckham, Giggs, Scholes, and the Neville brothers.
84. True or False: Manchester United have a women's team that competes in the Women's Super League.

- ○ True. The team was formed in 2018.
85. True or False: Manchester United's main rivals are Manchester City and Liverpool.

- ○ True. These rivalries are among the fiercest in English football.
86. True or False: The club's anthem is "Glory Glory Man

United."

- ○ True. This song is often sung by fans at matches.

87. True or False: Manchester United have a training ground called Carrington.

- ○ True. This is where the first team and academy players train.

88. True or False: The club has a statue of Sir Matt Busby outside Old Trafford.

- ○ True. The statue commemorates his contributions to the club.

89. True or False: Manchester United have a strong presence on social media.

- ○ True. The club has millions of followers on platforms like Twitter and Facebook.

90. True or False: Manchester United have been involved in several high-profile transfer deals.

- ○ True. The club has broken transfer records on several occasions.

Current Squad

91. True or False: Bruno Fernandes is the current captain of Manchester United.

    ○ True. He was appointed captain in July 2023.

92. True or False: Casemiro is a Brazilian midfielder who plays for Manchester United.

    ○ True. He joined the club in 2022.

93. True or False: Harry Maguire is a defender for Manchester United.

    ○ True. He joined the club in 2019.

94. True or False: Lisandro Martínez is an Argentinian defender who plays for Manchester United.

    ○ True. He joined the club in 2022.

95. True or False: Raphael Varane is a French defender who plays for Manchester United.

    ○ True. He joined the club in 2021.

96. True or False: Jadon Sancho is an English winger who plays

for Manchester United.

- ○ True. He joined the club in 2021.

97. True or False: Antony is a Brazilian winger who plays for Manchester United.

- ○ True. He joined the club in 2022.

98. True or False: Alejandro Garnacho is an Argentinian winger who plays for Manchester United.

- ○ True. He is a product of the club's academy.

99. True or False: Christian Eriksen is a Danish midfielder who plays for Manchester United.

- ○ True. He joined the club in 2022.

100.   True or False: David de Gea is a Spanish goalkeeper who plays for Manchester United.

- ● True. He has been with the club since 2011.

Chapter 2: Trivia Questions

Players

1. Who was the first Manchester United player to win the Ballon d'Or?

    o Answer: Denis Law (1964)

2. Which Manchester United player holds the record for most Premier League appearances?

    o Answer: Ryan Giggs (632 appearances)

3. Who scored the winning goal for Manchester United in the 1999 Champions League final?

    o Answer: Ole Gunnar Solskjaer

4. Which player is Manchester United's all-time leading goalscorer?

    o Answer: Wayne Rooney (253 goals)

5. Who was nicknamed "Captain Marvel" during his time at Manchester United?

- o Answer: Bryan Robson
6. Which Portuguese forward wore the number 7 shirt for Manchester United in two separate spells?

   - o Answer: Cristiano Ronaldo
7. Who was the first non-British or Irish player to captain Manchester United?

   - o Answer: Eric Cantona
8. Which goalkeeper holds the record for the most clean sheets for Manchester United?

   - o Answer: Peter Schmeichel (180 clean sheets)
9. Which player scored a hat-trick on his Manchester United debut in 2004?

   - o Answer: Wayne Rooney (against Fenerbahçe in the Champions League)
10. Which Manchester United player is known for his "kung-fu kick" incident in 1995?

    - o Answer: Eric Cantona

Stadiums

11. What is the nickname of Manchester United's home ground?

    ○ Answer: "The Theatre of Dreams" (given by Sir
      Bobby Charlton)

12. In what year did Manchester United move to Old Trafford?

    ○ Answer: 1910

13. What is the capacity of Old Trafford?

    ○ Answer: Approximately 74,000

14. Which stand at Old Trafford is known for housing the most
    vocal Manchester United supporters?

    ○ Answer: The Stretford End

15. Which two grounds did Manchester United play at before
    moving to Old Trafford?

    ○ Answer: Bank Street and North Road

Historical Moments

16. In what year did the Munich Air Disaster occur?

   o   Answer: 1958

17. In which year did Manchester United achieve the treble?

   o   Answer: 1999

18. Who was the manager when Manchester United won their first European Cup?

   o   Answer: Matt Busby

19. When did Manchester United win their first league title?

   o   Answer: 1908 (as Manchester United, after the name change from Newton Heath)

20. Which team did Manchester United beat in the 2008 Champions League final?

   o   Answer: Chelsea (after a penalty shootout)

Competition Rules

21. How many points does a team get for a win in the Premier League?

- ○ Answer: 3 points

22. How many teams are relegated from the Premier League each season?

- ○ Answer: 3 teams

23. How many substitutes are allowed in a Premier League match?

- ○ Answer: 5 substitutes (from a maximum of 9 named on the bench)

24. What is the name of the cup competition that features all 92 clubs from the Premier League and the English Football League?

- ○ Answer: The FA Cup

25. How many teams qualify from the Premier League for the Champions League?

- ○ Answer: The top 4 teams

English Football

26. Which team has won the most FA Cup titles?

  ○ Answer: Arsenal (14 titles)

27. Who is the all-time top scorer in the Premier League?

  ○ Answer: Alan Shearer (260 goals)

28. In what year was the Premier League founded?

  ○ Answer: 1992

29. Which English club won the first-ever Premier League title?

  ○ Answer: Manchester City (in the 1992-93 season)

30. Which trophy is contested between the winners of the Premier League and the FA Cup?

  ○ Answer: The FA Community Shield

Players (Continued)

31. Who was known as the "Ginger Prince" during his time at Manchester United?

● Answer: Paul Scholes

32. Which player famously wore the number 18 shirt for

Manchester United?

- Answer: Paul Scholes

33. Who was the first Manchester United player to score a hat-trick in the Premier League?

- Answer: Andrei Kanchelskis (against Sheffield Wednesday in 1995)

34. Which player scored the winning penalty for Manchester United in the 2008 Champions League final shootout?

- Answer: Edwin van der Sar

35. Which defender is known for his "no-look" passes?

- Answer: Lisandro Martínez

Stadiums (Continued)

36. What is the name of the tunnel at Old Trafford that commemorates the victims of the Munich Air Disaster?

  - Answer: The Munich Tunnel

37. Which stand at Old Trafford is named after Sir Alex Ferguson?

- Answer: The Sir Alex Ferguson Stand (formerly the North Stand)

38. Which three players are featured in the "United Trinity" statue outside Old Trafford?

- Answer: George Best, Denis Law, and Bobby Charlton

39. In what year did Old Trafford host the Champions League final?

- Answer: 2003

40. What is the name of the road on which Old Trafford is located?

- Answer: Sir Matt Busby Way

Historical Moments (Continued)

41. In what year did Manchester United win their first FA Cup?

- Answer: 1909

42. Who was the manager when Manchester United were relegated to the Second Division in 1974?

- Answer: Tommy Docherty

43. In what year did Eric Cantona make his debut for Manchester United?

- Answer: 1992

44. Which team did Manchester United beat to win the FA Cup in 1990?

- Answer: Crystal Palace (after a replay)

45. In what year did Manchester United win their first League Cup?

- Answer: 1992

Competition Rules (Continued)

46. How many teams compete in the Premier League?

- Answer: 20 teams

47. How many foreign players can be named in a Premier League starting lineup?

- Answer: There is no limit on the number of foreign players in a starting lineup.

48. What is the name of the rule that was used in European competitions to determine the winner of a two-legged tie if the aggregate score was level?

- Answer: The away goals rule (abolished in 2021)

49. How many yellow cards does a player need to receive in a Premier League season to be suspended for one match?

- Answer: 5 yellow cards

50. What happens if a Premier League match ends in a draw?

- Answer: Each team receives 1 point.

Players

51. Which Manchester United player won the first-ever PFA Young Player of the Year award?

   o   Answer: Lee Sharpe (1990-91 season)

52. Which Manchester United player holds the record for the most appearances in European competitions for the club?

   o   Answer: Ryan Giggs (158 appearances)

53. Who was the first Manchester United player to score a goal at the new Wembley Stadium?

   o   Answer: Louis Saha (in the 2007 FA Cup final against Chelsea)

54. Which player scored the winning penalty for Manchester United in the 2017 UEFA Europa League final shootout?

   o   Answer: Paul Pogba

55. Which Manchester United player was nicknamed "The Smiling Assassin"?

   o   Answer: Ole Gunnar Solskjaer

56. Which defender holds the record for the most expensive defender in the world when he signed for Manchester United

in   2019?

   ○ Answer: Harry Maguire

57. Which player was the first to score 100 Premier League goals for   Manchester   United?

   ○ Answer: Andy Cole

58. Which player scored a hat-trick for Manchester United in the 1999 FA Cup semi-final replay against Arsenal?

   ○ Answer: Dwight Yorke

59. Which Manchester United player was known for his "Cantona-esque" goal celebration, where he would stand still with   his   arms   outstretched?

   ○ Answer: Eric Bailly

60. Which Manchester United player was nicknamed "The Black Pearl"   during   his   time   at   the   club?

   ○ Answer: Dwight Yorke

Stadiums

61. What is the name of the statue of Sir Matt Busby located outside Old Trafford?

- Answer: The Sir Matt Busby Statue

62. Which stand at Old Trafford was the last to be developed?

- Answer: The Sir Alex Ferguson Stand (completed in 2012)

63. What is the name of the megastore located at Old Trafford?

- Answer: The Manchester United Megastore

64. Which events other than football matches have been held at Old Trafford?

- Answer: Rugby League matches, concerts, and boxing matches

65. What is the name of the bridge that connects Old Trafford with the Trafford Centre?

- Answer: The Sir Alex Ferguson Bridge

Historical Moments

66. In what year did Manchester United win their first-ever trophy?

   ○ Answer: 1908 (the FA Charity Shield)

67. Who was the manager when Manchester United won the Intercontinental Cup in 1999?

   ○ Answer: Sir Alex Ferguson

68. In what year did Manchester United win their first and only UEFA Cup Winners' Cup?

   ○ Answer: 1991

69. Which team did Manchester United beat to win the FA Cup in 1994?

   ○ Answer: Chelsea

70. In what year did Manchester United win their first and only FIFA Club World Cup?

   ○ Answer: 2008

Competition Rules

71. How many teams compete in the UEFA Champions League group stage?

   ○ Answer: 32 teams

72. What is the name of the competition that features the winners of the Champions League and the Europa League?

   ○ Answer: The UEFA Super Cup

73. How many substitutes are allowed in a Champions League match?

   ○ Answer: 5 substitutes (from a maximum of 12 named on the bench)

74. What is the name of the system used to determine which teams qualify for European competitions from the Premier League?

   ○ Answer: UEFA coefficient

75. What is the name of the rule that prevents a player from scoring directly from a throw-in?

   ○ Answer: A player cannot score directly from a throw-in.

English Football

76. Which team has won the most League Cup titles?

   ○ Answer: Liverpool (9 titles)

77. Who is the all-time top scorer for the England national football team?

   ○ Answer: Harry Kane

78. In what year did England last win a major international tournament?

   ○ Answer: 1966 (FIFA World Cup)

79. Which city hosted the 2013 Champions League final?

   ○ Answer: London (Wembley Stadium)

80. What is the name of the award given to the best young player in the Premier League each season?

   ○ Answer: The PFA Young Player of the Year

Players (Continued)

81. Which Manchester United player was nicknamed "The Welsh Wizard"?

  ○ Answer: Ryan Giggs

82. Which player scored the fastest hat-trick in Premier League history for Manchester United?

  ○ Answer: Dwight Yorke (against Arsenal in 1999, in 4 minutes and 30 seconds)

83. Which Manchester United player was known for his powerful free-kicks and his "dead-ball" expertise?

  ○ Answer: Cristiano Ronaldo

84. Which Manchester United player was the first to score 50 goals in a single season?

  ○ Answer: Denis Law (1963-64 season)

85. Which player was the first non-British or Irish player to captain Manchester United?

  ○ Answer: Eric Cantona

Stadiums (Continued)

86. What is the name of the trophy room located at Old Trafford?

   o   Answer: The Manchester United Trophy Room

87. Which stand at Old Trafford is known for its iconic cantilever roof?

   o   Answer: The Sir Alex Ferguson Stand

88. What is the name of the memorial garden located at Old Trafford that commemorates the victims of the Munich Air Disaster?

   o   Answer: The Munich Memorial Garden

89. In what year did Old Trafford host the Rugby League World Cup   final?

   o   Answer: 2013

90. What is the name of the conference and events centre located at   Old   Trafford?

   o   Answer: The Manchester Suite

Historical Moments (Continued)

91. In what year did Manchester United win their first FA Charity Shield?

   ○ Answer: 1908

92. Who was the manager when Manchester United won the FA Cup in 1948?

   ○ Answer: Matt Busby

93. In what year did Manchester United win their first and only European Cup Winners' Cup?

   ○ Answer: 1991

94. Which team did Manchester United beat to win the FA Cup in 1996?

   ○ Answer: Liverpool

95. In what year did Manchester United win their first and only FIFA Club World Cup?

   ○ Answer: 2008

Competition Rules (Continued)

96. How many teams are there in the English Football League Championship?

  o Answer: 24 teams

97. What is the name of the competition that features the top four teams in the Premier League at the end of the season?

  o Answer: There is no official competition for the top four teams, but they qualify for the UEFA Champions League.

98. How many substitutes are allowed in an FA Cup match?

  o Answer: Up to 7 substitutes can be named on the bench, and a maximum of 5 can be used.

99. What is the name of the rule that allows a goalkeeper to handle the ball within their own penalty area?

  o Answer: The goalkeeper can handle the ball within their own penalty area.

100. What is the name of the rule that prevents a player from impeding an opponent who is not in possession of the ball?

  o Answer: Obstruction

Chapter 3: Fill-in-the-Blank & Other Games

Club History

1. Manchester United was founded in ____. (Answer: 1878)

2. The club was originally known as ____. (Answer: Newton Heath LYR Football Club)

3. Manchester United's home ground is called ____. (Answer: Old Trafford)

4. Old Trafford is nicknamed "The ____ of Dreams." (Answer: Theatre)

5. The Munich Air Disaster occurred in ____. (Answer: 1958)

6. Sir Matt Busby led Manchester United to their first European Cup victory in ____. (Answer: 1968)

7. Manchester United were relegated to the Second Division in ____. (Answer: 1974)

8. Sir Alex Ferguson became manager of Manchester United in ____. (Answer: 1986)

9. The Glazer family acquired ownership of Manchester United in ____. (Answer: 2005)

10. Manchester United won the FIFA Club World Cup in ____. (Answer: 2008)

Famous Players

11. David Beckham wore the number ___ shirt. (Answer: 7)

12. Eric Cantona was known as "King _____." (Answer: Eric)

13. Ryan Giggs is nicknamed the "_____ Wizard." (Answer: Welsh)

14. Paul Scholes was known as the "_____ Prince." (Answer: Ginger)

15. Cristiano Ronaldo won the Ballon d'Or in _____. (Answer: 2008)

16. Wayne Rooney is Manchester United's all-time leading _____. (Answer: goalscorer)

17. Marcus Rashford campaigns against _____ poverty. (Answer: child)

18. Peter Schmeichel was a legendary _____ for Manchester United. (Answer: goalkeeper)

19. Roy Keane was known for his _____ temperament as captain. (Answer: fiery)

20. Denis Law was part of the "United _____" with Best and Charlton. (Answer: Trinity)

Trophies and Achievements

21. Manchester United have won the English top-flight league title a record ___ times. (Answer: 20)

22. United won the treble in _____. (Answer: 1999)

23. The treble consists of the Premier League, FA Cup, and _____. (Answer: Champions League)

24. Manchester United have won the FA Cup ___ times. (Answer: 12)

25. The club has won the League Cup ___ times. (Answer: 6)

26. Sir Alex Ferguson won ___ Premier League titles with Manchester United. (Answer: 13)

27. Manchester United won their first European Cup in _____. (Answer: 1968)

28. The club won the UEFA Cup Winners' Cup in _____. (Answer: 1991)

29. Manchester United won the UEFA Europa League in _____. (Answer: 2017)

30. The club won the Intercontinental Cup in _____. (Answer: 1999)

Iconic Moments and Matches

31. Ole Gunnar Solskjaer scored the winning goal in the _____ Champions League final. (Answer: 1999)

32. Ryan Giggs scored a memorable solo goal against _____ in the 1999 FA Cup semi-final. (Answer: Arsenal)

33. Wayne Rooney scored a spectacular overhead kick against _____ in 2011. (Answer: Manchester City)

34. Eric Cantona's "kung-fu kick" incident occurred in _____. (Answer: 1995)

35. The first match at Old Trafford was played against _____. (Answer: Liverpool)

36. Manchester United beat Chelsea in the _____ Champions League final on penalties. (Answer: 2008)

37. The Stretford End is known for housing the most _____ Manchester United supporters. (Answer: vocal)

38. The Munich Tunnel is a memorial at Old Trafford commemorating the victims of the _____. (Answer: Munich Air Disaster)

39. The statue of the United Trinity outside Old Trafford features Best, Charlton, and _____. (Answer: Law)

40. Manchester United played their home games at _____ during World War II. (Answer: Maine Road)

Managers

41. _____ was the manager of Manchester United during the

Munich Air Disaster. (Answer: Matt Busby)

42. _____ was the manager who brought Cristiano Ronaldo to Manchester United in 2003. (Answer: Sir Alex Ferguson)

43. _____ was the manager when Manchester United won the treble in 1999. (Answer: Sir Alex Ferguson)

44. _____ was the manager when Manchester United were relegated to the Second Division in 1974. (Answer: Tommy Docherty)

45. _____ was the first manager to win the Premier League title with Manchester United. (Answer: Sir Alex Ferguson)

46. _____ was the manager when Manchester United won the FA Cup in 2016. (Answer: Louis van Gaal)

47. _____ was the manager when Manchester United won the UEFA Europa League in 2017. (Answer: José Mourinho)

48. _____ was the caretaker manager who was later appointed permanently. (Answer: Ole Gunnar Solskjaer)

49. _____ was the interim manager appointed after Ole Gunnar Solskjaer's departure. (Answer: Ralf Rangnick)

50. _____ is the current manager of Manchester United. (Answer: Erik ten Hag)

Club Culture and Identity

51. Manchester United's nickname is the _____. (Answer: Red Devils)

52. The club's traditional colours are red, white, and _____. (Answer: black)

53. "_____ Glory Man United" is a popular chant among the club's supporters. (Answer: Glory)

54. The "_____ Babes" were a group of young Manchester United players in the 1950s. (Answer: Busby)

55. "_____ Time" refers to the tendency for Manchester United to score late goals under Sir Alex Ferguson. (Answer: Fergie)

56. The Class of '___ refers to a group of young Manchester United players who emerged in the 1990s. (Answer: 92)

57. Manchester United have a dedicated TV channel called _____. (Answer: MUTV)

58. Manchester United's main rivals are Manchester City and _____. (Answer: Liverpool)

59. The club's anthem is "_____ Glory Man United." (Answer: Glory)

60. Manchester United have a training ground called _____. (Answer: Carrington)

Premier League Era

61. The Premier League was formed in _____. (Answer: 1992)

62. Manchester United have won the Premier League title a record ___ times. (Answer: 13)

63. _____ holds the record for most Premier League appearances. (Answer: Ryan Giggs)

64. _____ is the Premier League's all-time leading goalscorer. (Answer: Alan Shearer)

65. The Premier League is broadcast in over ___ countries. (Answer: 200)

66. The first-ever Premier League goal for Manchester United was scored by _____. (Answer: Mark Hughes)

67. _____ scored a hat-trick against Sheffield Wednesday in 1995, the first in the Premier League for United. (Answer: Andrei Kanchelskis)

68. Cristiano Ronaldo won the Premier League Golden Boot in _____. (Answer: 2007-08)

69. _____ won the Premier League Golden Glove award a record five times with Manchester United. (Answer: Peter Schmeichel)

70. Manchester United have _____ been relegated from the Premier League. (Answer: never)

European Competitions

71. Manchester United have won the European Cup/Champions League ___ times. (Answer: 3)

72. The club won their first European Cup in _____. (Answer: 1968)

73. Manchester United beat Benfica in the _____ European Cup final. (Answer: 1968)

74. The club won the UEFA Cup Winners' Cup in _____. (Answer: 1991)

75. Manchester United beat Barcelona in the _____ UEFA Cup Winners' Cup final. (Answer: 1991)

76. The club won the UEFA Europa League in _____. (Answer: 2017)

77. Manchester United beat Ajax in the _____ UEFA Europa League final. (Answer: 2017)

78. The European Cup was renamed the Champions League in _____. (Answer: 1992)

79. The away goals rule was abolished in European competitions in _____. (Answer: 2021)

80. VAR (Video Assistant Referee) was introduced to the Champions League in _____. (Answer: 2019)

Miscellaneous

81. _____ is the name of the youth academy that has produced many Manchester United stars. (Answer: Manchester United Academy)

82. _____ is the current kit manufacturer for Manchester United. (Answer: Adidas)

83. _____ is the main shirt sponsor for Manchester United. (Answer: TeamViewer)

84. _____ is the name of the fanzine that has been published by Manchester United supporters since 1989. (Answer: Red Issue)

85. _____ is the name of the mascot for Manchester United. (Answer: Fred the Red)

86. _____ is the name of the song that is played when Manchester United score a goal at Old Trafford. (Answer: "Song 2" by Blur)

87. _____ is the name of the charity closely associated with Manchester United. (Answer: Manchester United Foundation)

88. _____ is the current women's team manager. (Answer: Marc Skinner)

89. The Manchester United women's team was formed in _____. (Answer: 2018)

90. Manchester United have a reserve team that plays in _____.

(Answer: Premier League 2)

Current Squad

91. _____ is the current captain of Manchester United. (Answer: Bruno Fernandes)

92. _____ is a Brazilian midfielder who plays for Manchester United. (Answer: Casemiro)

93. _____ is a French defender who plays for Manchester United. (Answer: Raphael Varane)

94. _____ is an English winger who plays for Manchester United. (Answer: Jadon Sancho)

95. _____ is a Brazilian winger who plays for Manchester United. (Answer: Antony)

96. _____ is an Argentinian winger who plays for Manchester United. (Answer: Alejandro Garnacho)

97. _____ is a Danish midfielder who plays for Manchester United. (Answer: Christian Eriksen)

98. _____ is a Spanish goalkeeper who plays for Manchester United. (Answer: David de Gea)

99. _____ is an English defender who plays for Manchester United. (Answer: Luke Shaw)

100.   _____ is a Scottish midfielder who plays for Manchester United. (Answer: Scott McTominay)

Matching Games

Game 1: Match the Player to their Jersey Number

- David Beckham - 7
- Eric Cantona - 7
- Cristiano Ronaldo - 7
- Wayne Rooney - 10
- Marcus Rashford - 10
- Paul Scholes - 18
- Ryan Giggs - 11
- Roy Keane - 16
- Peter Schmeichel - 1
- Nemanja Vidić - 15

Game 2: Match the Year to the Trophy Won

- 1968 - European Cup
- 1999 - Treble (Premier League, FA Cup, Champions League)
- 2008 - Champions League

- 2017 - UEFA Europa League

- 1991 - UEFA Cup Winners' Cup

- 1909 - FA Cup

- 1992 - League Cup

- 2013 - Premier League

- 2008 - FIFA Club World Cup

- 1999 - Intercontinental Cup

Game 3: Match the Manager to their Era

- Matt Busby - 1940s-1960s (and briefly in 1970-71)

- Tommy Docherty - 1970s

- Ron Atkinson - 1980s

- Sir Alex Ferguson - 1986-2013

- David Moyes - 2013-14

- Louis van Gaal - 2014-2016

- José Mourinho - 2016-2018

- Ole Gunnar Solskjaer - 2018-2021

- Ralf Rangnick - 2021 (interim)

- Erik ten Hag - 2022-present

Game 4: Match the Nickname to the Player

- "King Eric" - Eric Cantona

- "The Ginger Prince" - Paul Scholes
- "The Welsh Wizard" - Ryan Giggs
- "Captain Marvel" - Bryan Robson
- "The Baby-Faced Assassin" - Ole Gunnar Solskjaer
- "The White Pele" - Wayne Rooney
- "The Fifth Beatle" - George Best
- "The Black Pearl" - Dwight Yorke
- "The Great Dane" - Peter Schmeichel
- "Mr. Manchester United" - Sir Bobby Charlton

Game 5: Match the Stadium to its Significance

- Old Trafford - Current home ground
- Bank Street - Former home ground (1893-1910)
- North Road - First home ground (1878-1893)
- Maine Road - Temporary home ground during World War II
- Wembley Stadium - Hosted the 1968 European Cup final and 2003 Champions League final

Game 6: Match the Year to the Event

- 1908 - First league title
- 1958 - Munich Air Disaster
- 1968 - First European Cup triumph

- 1999 - Treble
- 2008 - Second Champions League triumph
- 2013 - Sir Alex Ferguson retires
- 2017 - UEFA Europa League triumph
- 1992 - Premier League founded
- 2005 - Glazer family takeover
- 2018 - Women's team formed

Game 7: Match the Goal to the Goalscorer

- The volley against Arsenal in the 1999 FA Cup semi-final - Ryan Giggs
- The overhead kick against Manchester City in 2011 - Wayne Rooney
- The last-minute winner in the 1999 Champions League final - Ole Gunnar Solskjaer
- The free-kick against Portsmouth in 2008 - Cristiano Ronaldo
- The chip goal against Sunderland in 1996 - Eric Cantona

Game 8: Match the Player to their Nationality

- Eric Cantona - French
- Ryan Giggs - Welsh
- Cristiano Ronaldo - Portuguese

- Wayne Rooney - English

- Peter Schmeichel - Danish

- Roy Keane - Irish

- Denis Law - Scottish

- Ruud van Nistelrooy - Dutch

- David Beckham - English

- Nemanja Vidić - Serbian

Game 9: Match the Trophy to the Number of Times Won

- Premier League titles - 13
- FA Cups - 12
- League Cups - 6
- Champions League titles - 3
- UEFA Europa League titles - 1

Game 10: Match the Term to its Definition

- Fergie Time - The tendency for Manchester United to score late goals under Sir Alex Ferguson
- Busby Babes - A group of young Manchester United players in the 1950s
- The Class of '92 - A group of young Manchester United

players who emerged in the 1990s

- The Stretford End - A stand at Old Trafford known for housing the most vocal United supporters
- The Theatre of Dreams - Nickname for Old Trafford

The contents of this book may not be copied, reproduced or transmitted without the express written permission of the author or publisher. Under no circumstances will the publisher or author be responsible or liable for any damages, compensation or monetary loss arising from the information contained in this book, whether directly or indirectly. .

Disclaimer Notice:

Although the author and publisher have made every effort to ensure the accuracy and completeness of the content, they do not, however, make any representations or warranties as to the accuracy, completeness, or reliability of the content. , suitability or availability of the information, products, services or related graphics contained in the book for any purpose. Readers are solely responsible for their use of the information contained in this book

Every effort has been made to make this book possible. If any omission or error has occurred unintentionally, the author and publisher will be happy to acknowledge it in upcoming versions.